Ghana On My Mind

GHANA ON MY MIND
Poetic Reflections on Journeying to the Motherland

Copyright © 2021 by Zakiyyah G.E. Capehart

All rights reserved. No part of this book may be used or reproduced in any manner whatsoever without the written permission of the author. The only exceptions are brief quotations embodied in critical articles or reviews.

Published by Book Power Publishing, a division of NIYAH.

Special discounts on bulk quantities of Book Power Books are available to corporations, professional associations, non-profit organizations, universities, and others.

Contact the author via www.sistahzakiyyah.com

Cover Photo by Bryant B. Bolling

The following poems were previously published by Pacific Raven Press, LLC, Ka'a 'awa, Hawai'i 96730, in "Our Spirits Carry Our Voices." 2019

Ghana, Oh Ghana; Stepping into my Elderhood at the Enslavement Dungeons; Greeted by a Rainbow; Meeting Prince Joey; Poetry Slam Prepping; The Poetry Slam (only part of The Poetry Slam)

ISBN 978-1-945873-26-3

Printed in the United States of America

www.bookpowerpublishing.com

Ghana On My Mind

Poetic Reflections on Journeying to the Motherland

ZAKIYYAH G.E. CAPEHART

BOOK POWER
DETROIT, MICHIGAN

Dedication

To my mother, Pollie Lee Smallwood-Capehart, for giving me the ingredients of life through her songs and affirmations.

Below is a poem entitled Reflections, which I wrote for my dearly beloved Mother, who has been the strength and backbone for my family. Mother, the family loves and salutes you.

mom is my mirror
as she has always been
i hold that mirror proudly
and give thanks for the blessing
because i still receive valuable lessons
that enhances my life beautifully
from a powerful, gentle, brilliant woman
who always has a proverb
for the challenges in life
a song to soften
the mysteries of life
a smile to encourage
my journey through life

Advance Praise for Ghana On My Mind

"Zakiyyah Capehart's book of poetry and prose is a love song of returning to our Motherland, Ghana, West Africa with a group of poets from Oakland CA. In Ghana they met local poets and rejoiced as only poets can do. Zakiyyah's poem and prose narrative is a tale of return through the door of no return, the dungeons of horrors called castles as she noted.

My daughter Muhammida El Muhajir is a resident of Accra and part of a movement called Blaxit, i.e., North American Africans who return to our Motherland permanently. Zakiyyah's book is a must read for any North American Africans visiting our Motherland. You will enjoy her poetic and prose notes on the Ghanaian people, culture and history".

MARVIN X, *Co-founder of the Black Arts Movement, poet, playwright, essayist, publisher Black Bird Press, Oaktown CA*
1/17/21

"This book you now hold in your hands is more than just another book of Poems & Stories. This book is a literary roadmap to a reclamation of the heart & soul of an African born in America. This book is Zakiyyah G. E. Capehart's love poem to Ghana, "a place where sunlight, moonlight & starlight are etched on the faces of the people." This is a book you will not be able to forget! So get comfortable & be ready to take a beautiful & educational journey home!!!"

Avotcja, *Writer/Musician*
KPOO-FM & KPFA-FM

"Ghana on My Mind is a poetic meditation by Zakiyyah G.E. Capehart that is rich with details of her life-changing travel to Ghana, West Africa. Together with the cohort of poets who make up the West Oakland to West Africa Poetry Exchange (WO2WA), Zakiyyah shares the exciting journey of reconnecting to the motherland. Through poems and narrative reflection, Zakiyyah charts the trajectory of her trip and celebrates the people and places she learns from during this experience. Culminating with the WO2WA Slam Championship Poetry Exchange with the Ghanaian Ehalakasa Poetry Group, Zakiyyah takes the reader right up on stage with her. Rooted in memory and ancestry, this book is a joyous celebration of diaspora."

Nia McAllister, *Poet and Founder of the MoAD Lit Open Mic*

""I'll Take You There!" by the Staple Singers, came to mind after reading "Ghana on My Mind." I was taken by this literary portal to the Motherland! I was also reminded of the local venue called A Taste of Africa, because Zakiyyah's book gave me a scrumptilicious Taste of Ghana. For all the senses, mind, spirit and soul, Ghana on My Mind is a delightful read, I must concede, it will make you plead: Gotta go to Ghana! Gotta go, go, go!!!"

Paradise Freejahlove Supreme, *Poet*

"Zakiyyah's 'Ghana on my Mind' not only brings the reader into her mind, but also into her eyes and soul. Her seamless transitions from reflections to prose to poetry flowed like the water our ancestors bathed in. I felt like I was there in Ghana with her and our WO2WA poet members all over again. The experience of this book is truly a gift to any reader ready to embrace Ghana on their mind."

Marcus "Adeshima" Lorenzo Penn, *M.D., C.Y.T., Self Care Restorative Coach, Self Care Reform Wellness*

Contents

Advance Praise for Ghana On My Mind	*vi*
Fun Facts About Ghana	*xi*
The Flag of Ghana	*xii*
Foreward	*xiii*
About This Book	*xvi*
Preparing For My Journey	1
Ghana – Oh, Ghana!	5
Ghana Welcomes Me	8
Stepping into My Elderhood at the Enslavement Dungeons	9
The Last Bath	12
My Path	14
He Carried Me	15
Village on Stilts	16
Ghanaian Fishing Village	21
The Sparkle in their Eyes	23
Greeted by a Rainbow	25
The Hole	28
Ghanaian Night Life	31
Market Day	33
Food that Warmed my Heart	38
Meeting Prince Joey	39
Poetry Slam Prepping	43
The Poetry Slam	45
Spirit of the Ghanaian People	50
Clear Like Water	52
Tomorrow's Leaders	54
On the Bus	56
The Billboards	57
Goodbye, Farewell, So Long	59
Ghana on My Mind	60
Acknowledgements:	*61*
Adinkra Symbols Used	*62*
About the Author	*64*

Fun Facts About Ghana

- Ghana is a democratically led West African country situated along the Gulf of Guinea and Atlantic Ocean.

- Bordered by the Ivory Coast, Burkina Faso, Togo and the Ocean

- 238,535 km2 or 92,099 sq mi

- Ghana means Warrior King in the Soninke language

- Gained independence in 1957

- Population: approximately 30 million

- Religion: 71.2% Christian, 17.6% Muslim, 5.2% traditional

- March 6 is the nation's Independence Day

- July 1 is celebrated as Republic Day

The Flag of Ghana

The flag of Ghana was adopted in 1957 and designed by Theodosia Salome Okoh

Red: The red represents the blood of those who died fighting in the country's struggle for independence

Gold: The gold represents Ghana's mineral wealth

Green: The green symbolizes the country's rich forests and natural wealth,

Black Star: The black star stands for the Ghanaian people and African freedom.

Foreward

A woman who stands tall in her power, Zakiyyah G.E. Capehart, artfully chronicles her journey to West Africa in her newest book, Ghana on my Mind. Rendered in prose and verse, her stories are deeply personal, and allow the reader to join her as she travels from Oakland to Accra, to Cape Coast and the El Mina Slave Dungeons, to Nzulezu a village on Lake Amansuri and back to Accra.

Known as the Slave Coast and the Gold Coast, Ghana has a history that is rich and controversial. For African Americans, the Sankofa journey (a return to the African Motherland) is deeply symbolic, as a wellspring of healing and rejuvenation as well as of pain and remembrance.

Both in her depiction of Cape Coast Castle and in her poem, "The Last Bath," Zakiyyah grieves over "pain from the enslavers' torture" felt by her ancestors. However, what is more impactful are the truths that follow her essay, "Stepping into My Elderhood at the Enslavement Dungeons."

She writes, "During the libation ceremony, we prayed and meditated while calling out their names. Seestah IMAHKÜS, our guide, asked for the eldest in the group to step forward and give homage to our ancestors."

Capehart brings the reader to this healing moment, by sharing her pain and her joy. Tangential to the Year of the Return, proclaimed by President Nana Akufo-Addo, in 2019. This return journey foreshadows the mass repatriation to Africa that we are witnessing in the Black Lives Matter and post George Floyd era. As Black people feel increasing tension and rising violence within the parameters of COVID-19 and far-right politics backed by conspiracy theories, this Ghanaian welcoming home of Black Americans and descendants of enslaved African peoples, many of whom departed from the coast of West Africa in the 1500's-1800's, feels like the closing of a circle. A full healing.

As I read her words flowing into another, what struck me was the connection she felt to the people she met, whether in "Meeting Prince Joey" or in tasting coconut milk cut freshly from a tree, or in "The Ghanaian Fishing Village."

The heart of this book are the people. It is in a pivotal moment, in the metaphorical "Hole," that Capehart emerges Whole. This collection is about roots and transformation as much as it is about healing and self-care. In Zakiyyah's own words, this spiritual journey is where she realized that her "spirit is entwined with (her) people on the African continent." This is the healing, the moment, and the rejoicing that Zakiyyah G.E. Capehart brings to you in this groundbreaking collection.

Karla Brundage,
Founding Director, West Oakland to West Africa

About This Book

Ghana On My Mind, is a testimony through poems and short stories reflecting on my experience traveling to the Motherland in 2018.

My journey to Ghana, West Africa was lead by Karla Brundage, founder of the West Oakland to West Africa Poetry Exchange (WO2WA). We were ten poet members traveling. The Ghanaian and Oakland poets met in Accra, the capital of Ghana. The WO2WA poets were focused on meeting the Ghanaian poets and collectively participating in the upcoming Poetry Slam.

Ghana On My Mind, is a reading experience that highlights the culture, customs, architecture, scenery, and of course the beautiful and friendly Ghanaian people.

This book is also a decoration to acknowledge the President of Ghana, West Africa, Nana Akufo-Addo's invitation to African people in the diaspora to return back to the Motherland. His invitation is entitled, "The Year Of Return."

I hope you will be inspired after reading my book, to research, study, and experience for yourself this beautiful West African country.

Zakiyyah G.E. Capehart

Ghana On My Mind

1

Preparing For My Journey

After decades of dreaming about visiting Mother Africa, my dream was finally coming to fruition. Heading all the way across the ocean, there were a multitude of things to do to prepare for my journey. Luckily, I was travelling with my West Oakland To West Africa Poetry Exchange (WO2WA) and Karla, the group's founder and leader was an immense help. From fundraising events to the awesome "What to Bring to Ghana" list she provided to the group, my preparation was eased.

Bryant, my husband, also helped a great deal to ensure I was well-equipped for my journey. He conducted extensive research on Ghana and shared all the useful information with me, as well as encouraged me to also do my own research. He also gave me a great travel book on Ghana. Moreover, my four sisters, brother, and mother were also instrumental in making sure I had what I needed for my sojourn. All the support given to me was undoubtedly a godsend.

Everything was in place, I received my visa to Ghana without a hitch, finished paying for my airline ticket, the room and board accommodations were set, tours organized, and the requisite immunizations complete. After all the i's were dotted and all the t's were crossed, and after all the hectic packing, finally, I was ready.

On May 15, 2018, the day of my trip, Bryant and I were at the San Francisco airport early. I checked into KLM (Air France) Airlines, then proceeded to the security area. I was a bit nervous about everything clearing security so I asked Bryant to stay just in case he would have to take anything back home. Everything cleared and I was on my way.

Now it was time to get to the gate. I needed a wheelchair, but there was a forty-five minute wait, so I decided to proceed to the gate on my own. After a little while, my back pain started kicking in. My carry-on luggage was quite heavy and I struggled in managing it. I realized

I didn't experience pain before even with a heavy luggage because Bryant had carried it for me. Thankfully, I made it to the gate where most of the other poets were waiting.

We stopped in Amsterdam for a six-hour layover. After what seemed to be a really long wait, they announced that it was now time to board the aircraft for the flight to Ghana. As we began boarding, Africans appeared suddenly from all directions to join the line that had started to form. There was a sea of Black folks getting on the plane. "They look like me," I thought. I was so uplifted, happy, and excited! My heart was singing and rejoicing from within. My body vibrated with dance movements unknown to me.

With two floors, our plane was HUGE! I felt at home and like everyone boarding the plane were a part of my community. Mother Africa had been beckoning me for many decades, and it got stronger every year that passed by. Now that I was finally on my way, I knew my ancestors were now rejoicing!

Left to Right: Zakiyyah, Karla, Tyrice

Ghana – Oh, Ghana!

traveling by air
across the sea
journey of a lifetime
finally coming to be
land of my ancestors
history awaits
unveiling roots
opening wounds
where scars
are left to heal
weaving spirits
and touching souls
Ghana - Oh Ghana
constantly on my mind
when i arrive
what do i hope to find
will you be there

waiting to welcome
and receive me
with embracing arms
will i feel your love
running through me
until my cup
runneth over
here i sit
staring out at clouds
silently praying
Ghana - Oh Ghana
your distant disconnected family
is now returning home
to a country
once thought of as
the Land - Of - No - Return

WO2WA at Door of Return

Ghana Welcomes Me

my fanfare were the people
who all looked like me
beautifully smiling graciously
were they really smiling at me
i felt so accepted
from folks i didn't know
they approached warmly
giving information and direction
respectful
polite
genuine
i thought this must be heaven
had i arrived
feeling the love
gently holding me
this was the moment i imagined
being lovingly embraced

2

Stepping into My Elderhood at the Enslavement Dungeons

Photo: 1 Ancestral Altar in the Dungeon

We visited the Enslavement Dungeons, and it was absolutely heart-wrenching to see where our ancestors were held captive. In Ghana, on the Atlantic Ocean, right on the beautiful coasts of El Mina and Cape Coast, the Europeans built the dungeons and called them castles.

In those extremely small, dark and damp dungeons, our ancestors were chained, shackled, and locked up. The only light that entered from the outside was through a tiny hole on the ground level. Hundreds of Africans were packed on top of one another in these dungeons, where they ate, defecated, and slept. They did not receive any sunshine, adequate air, or exercise. Then after months of stewing in those horrible prisons, they were thrown into the bowels of a ship sailing to a new country.

I walked around the tiny space that used to cage hundreds of our ancestors. There were only ten of us in our group and yet, even we had barely enough space to move around. I looked closely at the inhumane rock-hard walls, floor, and ceiling. I imagined their suffering. My eyes swelled with water, but I was so overwhelmed with shock that my tears didn't fall.

We knew the ancestors were present. We visited with their spirits and shared the food we brought to feed them. During the libation ceremony, we prayed and meditated while calling out their names. Seestah IMAHKÜS, our guide, asked for the eldest in the group to step forward and give homage to our ancestors. Being the eldest, I stepped forward. I didn't know I would be called upon to speak and I had no idea what to say. Yet, the words came and flowed effortlessly from my mouth.

Honoring our ancestors was a spiritual epitome for me; an auspicious moment in time. I was very blessed and very thankful to have such privilege and freedom.

Photo: 2 The River where Ancestors took the "last bath"

The Last Bath

It was now time for the last bath. I followed the path my ancestors would had taken to have their bath in Ghana. Knowing each time my feet touched the ground, the spirits of my Ghanaian ancestors knew of my return. The sun shone on me through tall, bending, twin weeping trees. I felt their spiritual presence. The tranquility of the surroundings hushed my rebelliousness. Then finally, the tears that had been forming in my eyes rushed to escape down my cheeks. The path ceased at the water stream where they had bathed. I imagined how, after that bath, chained and shackled, they were made to walk for days to reach the ships.

Earlier that day, I had gone through a sermon of tragedy. I watched a film footage of how barbaric my ancestors were treated by the enslavers on the ships sailing to the New World. I felt their pain from the enslavers' torture. I grieved over and over for my ancestors as I watched that film. I cried like I had never cried before. My heart throbbed and felt as though it would burst from such horror.

I wanted it to be merely a nightmare.

But I knew all too well that it was true and those atrocious things had really happened to my ancestors.

These bloodcurdling films are hard to watch; these stories are unbearable to hear about, and impossible to imagine. However, even though this truth deeply hurts, we must continue to share and reveal these stories. It is an important part of history that must never be forgotten.

My Path

emotions run up and down my spine

like the growth of grapes on the vine

symbolic of veins

telling the stories of

hidden suppression

unveiling lost centuries

unmasked and exposed

Zakiyyah writing on Iconic Wall after visiting the River where Ancestors took the "last bath"

He Carried Me

the tide did rise
we climbed into a small boat
to get to the other side
upon arriving
we noticed the tide had risen
too much water
to step off the boat i summarize
with a glance of my eyes
a small Ghanaian boy said
"get on my back i will take you across"
he looked too small to carry me
but i took a chance
and in spite of my doubt
with amazing strength
he carried me on his back
happily   proudly   safely
to the other side

4

Village on Stilts

WO2WA poets arriving at the Village on Stilts

We, the West Oakland To West Africa Poetry Exchange, exited the bus and gathered around young Ghanaian men with small boats. They were our guides. The Village on Stilts, named Nzulezu, was our destination.

Nzulezu is located on Lake Amansuri in the Amansuri Wetland, which is the largest inland swamp forest in Ghana. Near the border of Côte d'Ivoire, the entire village is constructed from raffia (palm trees) and sits on wooden stilts.

The boat ride to Nzulezu on Lake Amansuri was serene, calm, and peaceful. One of the highlights of our travel, our guide regaled us with his historical narrative as we cruised and took in the exotic beauty of the lake. We passed through narrow and wide channels and saw lovely lush open plains. Vibrant greenery lined the shore. An array of colorful flowers peeped out at us like some hidden treasure, beckoning to be acknowledged.

Although rain wasn't in the forecast, a light shower sprinkled us briefly before arriving at the village.

As we disembarked, we were met and greeted warmly by a villager who turned out to be our guide. One long street, known as "Main Street" by the villagers, runs from one end of the village to the other. Homes and businesses line both sides. The school was at the far end of the village. I was certain this location allowed the students to concentrate much better on their school work, especially during the tourist season.

The Community Center was located in the middle of the village, making it very accessible to the villagers and tourists. A marketplace featuring beautiful wood-carved art, paintings, jewelry, and much more sits at the village entrance. Before we properly began the tour of the village, our group stopped by a store that sold refreshments—we were parched after the long bus and boat ride.

While walking along Main Street, we greeted many villagers who were busy working at home and tending their business. We saw the newly installed communal showers, which our guide said were a great addition to the village.

Their school, although small, provides the necessary education for the children. However, the village was in need of finances to purchase books and pay the teachers they hire. Our guide explained that the teachers sent by the government do not tend to stay, so the village has to continually hire new teachers to replace those who leave.

At the Community Center, some of the village elders talked to us about how the village continues to sustain itself. We, the WO2WA poets, made a financial donation to the further development of Nzulezu, especially to help them with the challenges they faced. It was an honor to be able to contribute in a meaningful way for a very worthy community.

Zakiyyah with Ghanaian man that caught and cut her fresh coconut

The Coconut Tree

never had a coconut
straight from the tree
a young boy said
he'd get one for me
up he climbed
courageously
gallantly
swiftly
down he came
coconut in hand
machete cut it
and gave me
my first drink
of fresh coconut water
soooooo refreshing
delicious and energizing
fruit smooth soft easy
melted in my mouth

5

Ghanaian Fishing Village

Our supposed visit to a Ghana beach in Accra had been rescheduled quite a few times. When the visit finally went through, we found that all the effort was worth it. As soon as we got there, we placed our lunch orders in a café that reminded me of a fish-and-chips place I used to frequent in Harlem, New York. The delectable aromas emanating from the wild freshly caught fish tantalized my palate and gave me a deeper appreciation of my sense of smell. That Harlem café could not hold a candle to the fresh fish at this Ghanaian café.

While we waited for our food to arrive, we talked over the rest of our plans in Accra before we'd head for Cape Coast. Some of us decided to take a stroll along the shore. Tyrice and Nate found a scenic spot on the rocks facing the ocean, where they stopped and sat to enjoy Ghana's beautiful ocean view.

Adeshima and I preferred to walk, dodging the waves along the way. Soon we arrived at a Ghanaian fishing village, just when the fishermen and women were returning with their morning catch. They exhibited wonderful cooperation and collective camaraderie as they got the boats on shore. Whenever a boat would come in, the people on the shore would gather and pull the boat out of the water. Their rhythm and timing were amazingly in sync. It was astonishing to watch. When the nets were pulled from the boat and dropped on the shore, they were bursting with hundreds of fish.

The boats were constantly arriving. The villagers were unrelenting in assisting one another. The children played and worked alongside the adults. There was jovial conversation and laughter, and so much love and respect. Watching them inspired me beyond my expectations.

After frolicking along the beach shore, we walked back to join the other poets for lunch. I smiled reflecting on my lovely day. I was so smitten by the experience that I would not have minded spending the day on the beach just savoring the seafood. Then I submerged myself into the ocean and enjoyed jumping the waves.

The Sparkle in their Eyes

watching the Ghanaian children play
made me smile
gave me such delight
their willingness
readiness
availability
to lend strangers
a helping hand
even when money
is not expected
seeing the children's
enthusiastic
eager
sparkling eyes and accepting smiles
hearing their cheerful joyous laughter
solidifies the spirituality and
connectiveness

Zakiyyah G.E. Capehart

in the culture between
Africans on the continent and
African Americans in the diaspora

Zakiyyah with Ghanaian youth at the beach

Greeted by a Rainbow
(previous title: The Place I Am From)

i come from a place
where greeting is paramount
a place where the moon
appears full each night
a place where the darkness
highlights zillions of stars
that kiss the sky
and brighten our path
through thickness in the woods
at the midnight hour
a place where the doors
are never locked
even as you sleep
a place where dew-drops halt
on the first note
the songbird sings

Zakiyyah G.E. Capehart

a place where porch swings
sing a lullaby to passersby
a place where summer breezes
soothe your sneezes
a place where neighbors talk
and children walk to play
in the early morning sun
greeted by a rainbow
i come from a place where
sunlight moonlight and starlight
are etched on the faces of the people
and shine throughout the universe
i come from a place where
pyramids are erected
in the enfolds of the
cerebrum cerebellum and medulla
i come from a place where
experiencing bitter hot sour and sweet
are precursors to life's journey

i come from a place where
greeting is a way of life
it begins and never ends

6

The Hole

After hearing that there was a nightclub a short walk from our hostel in Accra, Obe, Wanda, and I decided to visit it. We were not familiar with the area and were merely following Karla's directions. She said we'd have no trouble at all in finding the nightclub. After a short walk, we arrived at the corner where the nightclub was supposed to be. We heard music emanating from somewhere. Smiling as we nodded to the beat, we were sure the nightclub was near. However, as we looked up and down the street, there was no nightclub in sight. We tried to walk in the opposite direction, but the fading music told us it was not the right way. We kept walking and walking down streets that seemed to get darker and darker. That moment made me remember how North Carolinians often referred to a road that never comes to an end as a "country mile." The more you walk, the more there was to walk. Or so it seemed.

In the near distance, we saw a man. Obe said he would walk ahead of us to inquire about the night club. He walked in front of us progressively picking up his pace. Wanda and I walked slower, that way the man wouldn't be nervous with three strangers approaching him. When he returned, he informed us that there wasn't a nightclub in the direction we were going.

Now, we felt confident turning around would take us to our destination. As we approached the busy traffic street, we expected to hear music. But then we saw a man sitting on the side of the road with a music box. We realized that his music box was probably the source of the music that we had heard earlier.

I was walking slightly ahead of Wanda and Obe when suddenly, I fell into a hole. I tried to get up but couldn't—my body felt jumbled and contorted. Perplexed, shocked, and stunned I lay there in the hole. The street was null of lights. I knew Wanda and Obe were looking for me. I could hear them talking, but I was unable to respond.

Wanda said, "Zakiyyah, where are you?"

Obe said, "Where did she go?"

Thankfully, the next thing I knew, my friends were pulling me out of the hole. At that moment we didn't know how very fortunate I actually was.

Unbeknown to us, just a few steps ahead of me was an enormously deep hole, with no visible bottom. The thought of me disappearing at the blink of an eye, while Obe and Wanda walked only a few steps behind was bewildering. If I had missed the first hole and fell into the second hole, I might not be telling this story.

Luckily, I realized I wasn't seriously injured. To avoid any other possible accidents, we decided to hail a taxi and we finally made it to the nightclub, where all the other poets had been having a blast. We enjoyed a fabulous evening of live music and dancing outdoors under radiant stars, highlighting the beautiful Ghana sky.

Ghanaian Night Life

*my body glided
across the spacious
unbridled environment
granting me the ability
to feel feather-like
dancing to Ghanaian rhythms
the stage the band played upon
vibrated from music sounding
extraordinarily exhilarating
dancing outside under the stars
surrounded by a luminous
blackened sky
gave me an appreciation
of nightclubbing
i had not experienced before
dancing to the beat*

as i moved my feet
gifted me the freedom
i found in Ghana

7

Market Day

When we were asked on what day we wanted to go to the market, I was silent. When the other poets were deciding which market excited them most, I was silent. I was quiet because I wasn't planning to go to the market.

Unlike most women, I detest shopping. Where I am from women absolutely crave shopping. In fact they are obsessed with it. I on the other hand think it's a waste of precious time and money. I also think it could be considered a disease. Habitual shopping allows some people to obtain and remain wealthy; while others are barely able to stay alive.

As an African American woman, I speak of the culture in the USA that drives this behavior. I make it a point to only shop when necessary. However, when our group's market day arrived, I decided to go with the group. We were to stop at the Art Market first, then the Makola Market, Ghana's largest renowned marketplace and shopping district located in the center of Ghana's capital, Accra.

Some of the poets wanted to stay at the Art Market, but most wanted to visit both. I initially intended to stay at the Art Market, but curiosity got to me so I changed my mind and decided to explore both markets. This wise decision resulted in giving me knowledge I could only possibly receive in the Motherland.

Shopping in the land of my ancestors was a genuine cultural occasion. The no-frills sidewalk shops, mostly owned and operated by indigenous Ghanaian women, are filled with luxurious fabrics, clothing, jewelry, and other fine wares. An array of red, lavender, pink, black, brown, orange, white, green, and a multitude of other colors can be seen for miles from shop to shop. The stunning garments graced the market like an captivating home-grown dance.

The market was also a great place to enjoy the local food. The hustle and bustle were a joy to watch, too, as we mingled with shoppers dressed in extravagant clothing, reminiscent of the fine lavish dressing styles of African

Americans during the Harlem Renaissance.

The poets were paired together in groups of two and three, each group headed by a guide. Adeshima, Wanda, and I were in the same group. Our guide was a young Ghanaian man that worked at the hostel where we were staying. My roommate, Makeda, and I had had an opportunity to have a lovely conversation with him one evening at the hostel. He turned out to be a great guide at the market as well.

Wanda, Adeshima, and I were looking to purchase gifts for our family. We were also keeping an eye out to buy something for ourselves. Wanda needed some white fabric and bought a lovely piece for a great price. Adeshima was in search of Dashikis and discovered a couple of attractive ones that he purchased for a really good price, too. I saw two gorgeous dresses I wanted, but the seller was charging more for the dresses than I could pay. I told her I would buy both dresses for a lower price. We negotiated prices for a while until we agreed on what was acceptable. I was only going to buy one dress, but after haggling with the seller, she agreed to lower the price, enabling me to purchase both of the dresses.

The purchasing process at the market is a fact and a point of interest as well. The shop owner quotes a price, then the customer suggests a lower price. This could go on for a while, until the owner and customer agree on a price that satisfies them both. Sometimes, as a customer walks away, the shop owner would call out a lower price to get them back on the negotiating table.

It is empowering to have a voice in purchasing clothing and such. One can literally spend the entire day at the market treasuring the unique sounds and sights. An exceptional experience, market day should not be missed!

Ghana On My Mind

Beautiful market woman selling fruit

Ankara fabric hanging in market.jpg

Food that Warmed my Heart

food fit for kings and queens
enjoyed by everyone
if you know what i mean
light soup with fufu
was my favorite dish
then i tried "red red"
a fine bean curry
and changed my mind
but after cassava and plantains
i could not decide
the food kept coming
banku and pepper / okra stew
a dish to die for
became my new love
angwa muu / local jollof rice
added the touch that
completely warmed my heart

8

Meeting Prince Joey

The West African poets were coming to visit us, the West Oakland poets, at our hostel. We were all busy preparing for their arrival. However, we didn't know if they would actually make it, because it was raining so hard. It was as if billions of buckets of water were being poured simultaneously from the sky. There was also a lot of flooding taking place in Accra that day. But what we didn't take into account was the fact that Ghanaians were used to this heavy rainy season and all the flooding it brought. And so, true to their word, our West African poet partners showed up.

The day we all finally met was most joyous! I met my Ghanaian poet partner, Prince Joey. We excitedly embraced and hugged each other. It reminded me of the family reunions I experienced with my biological family. Prince Joey and I were both very happy to meet in person. We had already met online. Our groups had shared poetry on Skype, and he and I had been writing poems to each other for approximately a year. The two of us embraced and hugged for a long while. He is of my grandson's age. Therefore, it felt like I was meeting another grandson for the first time. We held on as if we'd lose each other if we let go. Standing up, we talked a long time. Then we sat down beside each other and continued to chat.

One of six sons in his family, Prince Joey and his twin brother are the youngest of the siblings. He is a twenty-one-year-old college student who also works at a restaurant. Other than being a poet, Prince Joey is also a filmmaker and actor. During our conversation, he told me about the film he made with a couple of his friends, including Emmanuel Akambo, a poet member of the

group. He said the film was to premiere that weekend. I was very excited to be in Ghana during his film viewing, so I asked him to announce his film to the group. When he informed the others, they were interested and wanted to go. We adjusted our schedule so we could attend.

The film was an interesting comedy, and we laughed a lot. It was shown outdoors on an enchanting Ghana evening, in an intimate garden setting. I enjoyed witnessing another aspect of my poet partner's creativity. Prince Joey is a respectful, conscientious Ghanaian young man. I'm glad we were chosen to be poet partners, to build fires in our writing.

Zakiyyah & Prince Joey at Poetry Slam

Agoo Hostel... the poets meet

9

Poetry Slam Prepping

The main reason for the our group's journey to Ghana was the poetry slam and it had arrived at last. Not only do we get to perform our poetry for the Ghanaian audience, we'd also get to perform with our poet partner.

The poetry slam was scheduled to begin at 6:29PM at the W.E.B. DuBois Memorial Centre, a short distance from where we were staying. The W.E.B. DuBois Memorial Centre is a historical, educational, and spiritually inspiring center. It left a deep impression on the group after we visited it earlier that week, so we thought it would be amazing to be there again!

Since our event would take place in the evening, we had most of the day to prepare ourselves. What poems should I recite? Should I wear a dress or pants? The locks of my hair were uniquely styled up crowning my head. I considered taking them down, but I changed my mind when I realized it would be a monumental task.

But performing in the poetry slam, which we had been planning for a year, made me edgy. I wondered how we would be received by an unfamiliar audience, on a different continent. Will they like our poetry? Although my roommate, Makeda, seemed relaxed and confident, it occurred to me that the other poets may also be having the same pre-performance jitters. I couldn't find Wildflower, Imani, and Xiomara, who were also staying on the second floor as I was, so I didn't know how they were feeling. I had not also spoken with the poets on the first floor, namely Karla, Wanda, Tyrice, and Adeshima (aka, Marcus). Before long, Karla came upstairs looking a little stressed out. She said some of the poets were having difficulty selecting their poems.

I needed a secluded area to select and practice my poems. Then I recalled the perfect spot: an outdoor porch area in the back. I had gone there a couple of times, to be alone. No one was ever there. So I used that space to prepare myself. The WO2WA Slam Championship Poetry Exchange Project with Ehalakasa awaits.

The Poetry Slam

The WO2WA poets took several taxis to reach the poetry slam. When we arrived, the students from the Ghanatta Performing Arts High School in Dodowa, where we had earlier conducted a workshop, were already performing their play. Even though we missed some of it, what we caught was wonderful!

The students articulated beautifully. Their costumes were creatively designed and brilliantly colored. Their dedication and discipline to their project spoke volumes. It was refreshing to see, and delightful to witness and enjoy the artistry of the Ghanaian students.

For our performances, it was decided that each poet would select a number from a pool of numbers, lottery style, to determine in what order we would perform.

One of the taxi drivers got lost enroute to the venue. We poets were concerned whether the driver would arrive soon with the poet being transported in that vehicle.

I selected a slip of paper with the number "2" on it. I really wanted to perform first so that as soon as I was finished, I could take a seat in the audience, relax and watch the other poets perform. However, being the second poet on stage gave me fundamentally the same opportunity. Furthermore, I had not participated in a poetry slam before and I was a bit anxious. My perception of what a poetry slam involved contributed to my nervousness. Frankly, I just wanted to quickly get my performance done and over with.

I had no idea how this event would change my opinion about poetry slams. I was so excited about my experience. In fact, once I returned to Oakland, I couldn't wait to find and participate in other poetry slams.

Finally, the lost taxi arrived. We poets all lined up near the stage, according to our respective number. It was a beautiful evening. The lights glared at the stage, which was spacious and somewhat intimidating. But the people in the packed audience were eagerly anticipating the show, and their excitement reassured us and made us feel supported.

Our long-awaited moment had come into fruition. The West Oakland to West Africa Poetry Exchange Group and the Ehalakasa Poetry Group began by reciting poetry with their poet partner. This demonstrated the Renshi style of poetry that the two groups wrote in, and exchanged poetry with each other for about a year. Renshi is a Japanese style of poetry creation where a poet writes a poem and sends it to another poet. The receiving poet takes the last line of the sender's poem to begin their poem.

It was time for the slam to begin. For this part of the program there is audience participation. Each poet had three minutes to perform, during which time no props or assistance from other people was allowed or the poet would be disqualified. Each poet, who must abide by the set rules of the slam, received individual points from the voting audience. After all the poets performed and received their points, the individual points were then calibrated for each group and an overall score per group was obtained.

The group with the highest score was the winner, and the winning team would receive a prize. The entire process was quick, fun, competitive, and exhilarating. In the end, the Ehalakasa Group won the poetry slam, but only by a single point.

This was the WO2WA's first international performance on the African continent. In addition, it was the first collective poetry slam with the Ehalakasa poet partners. I felt like henceforth, the groups would be on the map. There would be no stopping us now!

Poetry Groups (WO2WA & Ehalakasa) on Stage at Poetry Slam

11

Spirit of the Ghanaian People

It has been said that, "home is where the heart is." Traveling to Ghana was an experience of a lifetime. When I arrived there, I felt like I had returned home. The weight of stress lifted off me as an indescribable calm rendered me speechless. I realized my spirit is entwined with my people on the African continent.

My outlook on life had changed, even as I returned to Oakland. I can only say that while I am physically here in North America, I am still in Africa spiritually. For two weeks after my trip, my dreams were all about the beautiful Ghanaian people. Now my daily meditations take me back to the Ghana oceanside. I can feel the presence of the azure ocean, with the air and sun soothing my body, as it did when I was there. The Motherland had been calling me for decades. I felt very blessed to have arrived at last.

In Accra during the early morning, I would hear the Muslim call to prayer. The lovely prayers were like spiritual music that touched my soul. The silence surrounding the environment elevated the prayers of love and peace. I rejoiced in the rebirthing womb of Blackness awaiting a new day coming forth.

Clear Like Water

i meditate by Ghana's ocean
embracing my culture
celebrating with family
speaking my native language
i thought i'd forgotten
but it's in my DNA
where nothing is lost
just lying dormant
awaiting acknowledgement
to rise again
from my ocean within

Tomorrow's Leaders

the attentive articulate inquisitive
high school students
were refreshing to witness
their openness in sharing
patience to listen
thoughts about life
creative ideas for change
sensibility and sensitivity
towards others
as well as their awareness of
local community challenges
and worldly issues, too,
has opened the door
giving tomorrow's leaders
the opportunity to
seek and explore

WO2WA and Ghanatta H.S. students pose for photo

On the Bus

Circumstances dictated limited quarters. However, commuting by bus gave us poets an opportunity to delve, inquire, and discover more about Ghana. On those commutes, we poets also got to know each other a little better... we talked a lot. Sometimes, we ate more than we talked. On longer bus rides, like traveling from Accra to Cape Coast, we got to catch up on some much-appreciated rest because napping was part of the agenda as well. But in the end, we all developed a family-like closeness with one another.

Essentially, observing and conversing with Ghanaians, enjoying the country's breathtaking sights, and taking notice of the changing architecture gave us an understanding of Ghana we'd never gain in the USA. The panoramic view from the bus showed the country's raw natural beauty. Traveling to and around Ghana was an invaluable education—one that will live forever in my memory.

The Billboards

traveling by bus
it was marvelous to see
on every billboard
the people looked like me
i kept watching
if this scenario
would change
because where i live
the difference
creates pain
too sad to explain
the billboards
from the bus windows
gave me such delight
i emerged in wonderment
instead of fright
looking at faces

of Black people
on billboards
riding along the highway
made me feel proud
elevated my self-esteem
connected me closer
to the Ghanaian people
and my ancestors

Goodbye
Farewell
So Long

when it was time to go

i wanted to know

was it really already time

and was i saying

goodbye

farewell

or so long

parting felt like leaving a friend

i desired to stay

but knew my journey

had come to an end

feeling torn within

i hold on to my memories

until i return again

Ghana on My Mind

Dear Ghana,

Throughout the day, I think of you constantly when I meditate and pray, and even while I play. You have become a beautiful part of my daily thoughts.

I miss the ocean, the waves, the gentle breeze, the warmth of the sun, and the brilliant, stunning, beauteous stars covering the black sky at night.

Of course, I miss the scrumptious, delightful, aromatic food, as well as a mélange of other things. However, what I miss most of all are your people.

I am drawn to return to you. I know one day I shall—although, in spirit, I never really left you. In spirit, I am still there, enjoying the warmth of your sun, forever dreaming under your stars. Ghana is in my heart. Ghana is in my soul. Ghana is on my mind, nearly all the time.

Love,
Zakiyyah

Acknowledgements:

I am profoundly grateful to my husband, Bryant B. Bolling, who listened to my poems and stories during the creating, rewriting, and editing of this book.

A special thank you to my family for their support in my travel to Ghana, West Africa.

Adinkra Symbols Used

Throughout the book you will find beautiful African symbols known as adinkra. These symbols of the Akan people are used to decorate cloth, walls, pottery and more. Each symbol represents and idea or word central to life. I've selected seven to share here.

Gye Nyame
the supremacy of God

Adinkrahene
Greatness, charisma and leadership

Sankofa
The importance of learning from the past.

Fawohodie
independence, freedom and emancipation

Funtunfunefu Denkyemfunefu
democracy and unity

Nyansapo
wisdom, ingenuity, intelligence and patience

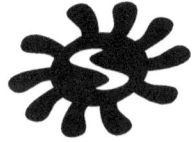
Bi Nka Bi
Peace and harmony

About the Author

Zakiyyah G.E. Capehart is a writer, published poet, storyteller, performance artist, visual artist, and radio producer and host. Zakiyyah's poetry is published in many anthologies. Her radio shows are aired on KPFA in Berkeley, CA. She combines her artistic skills and medical background, producing shows to educate and heal the community. Zakiyyah has been granted funds several times from the Akonadi Foundation, to write and perform productions to address community awareness in Oakland. In 2018, Zakiyyah travelled to Ghana, West Africa with the West Oakland to West Africa Poetry Exchange (WO2WA). While in Ghana, the group participated in a Poetry Slam with Ghanaian poets. Born in North Carolina, her family migrated to New York City when she was a child. Zakiyyah currently resides with her husband Bryant in Oakland, CA.

zakiyyahgecapehart@gmail.com

Sistahzakiyyah.com

Notes

www.ingramcontent.com/pod-product-compliance
Lightning Source LLC
Chambersburg PA
CBHW041131110526
44592CB00020B/2765